THE BATTLE OF GAINSBOROUGH
1643

THE BATTLE OF GAINSBOROUGH 1643

JOHN WEST

First published 2021 by DB Publishing, an imprint of JMD Media Ltd, Nottingham, United Kingdom.

ISBN 9781780916187

Printed in the UK

CONTENTS

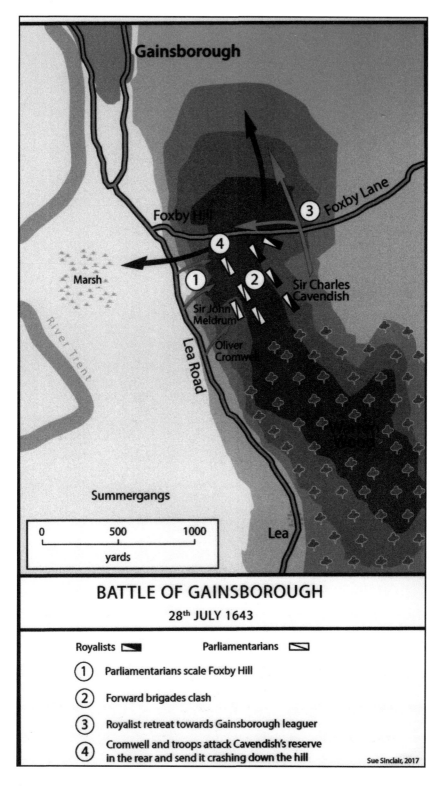

BATTLE OF GAINSBOROUGH
28th JULY 1643

Royalists | **Parliamentarians**

① Parliamentarians scale Foxby Hill

② Forward brigades clash

③ Royalist retreat towards Gainsborough leaguer

④ Cromwell and troops attack Cavendish's reserve in the rear and send it crashing down the hill

Sue Sinclair, 2017

PREFACE AND ACKNOWLEDGEMENTS

THE ENGLISH Civil War was one of the bloodiest events in our history. It has been estimated that England suffered a 3.7 per cent loss of population as a direct result of the conflict. The suffering in Scotland and Ireland was even greater with losses of 6 per cent and 41 per cent respectively. This is in contrast to the 3 per cent of the British population that later died in World War One.

Gainsborough was very much on the front line at the outbreak of hostilities and was unable to remain neutral as many in the town had hoped. The years 1643 and 1644 would see Gainsborough fought over several times by both king and parliament. It would also play a small but important part in the rise of the man who was to destined to replace Charles I as head of state – Oliver Cromwell.

This is the story of the Battle of Gainsborough and the events that led to it.

I would like to thank the following people for their help in compiling this book: Rosie Evans for proofreading the original manuscript; Sue Sinclair for designing the map of the battlefield; Professor Martyn Bennett for allowing me to use the map and for writing the introduction; Kevin Winter and Don Smith of the Battlefield Trust for writing the foreword and Jason Figgis for designing the front cover.

INTRODUCTION
BY PROFESSOR MARTYN BENNETT

JOHN WEST'S 1992 booklet *Oliver Cromwell and the Battle of Gainsborough* provided overdue coverage of important events in the history of the town, but it brought to wider public attention a milestone in the career of Oliver Cromwell.

In popular imagination, the mid-17th century civil wars were an English affair: a battle between King Charles I and parliament led by Oliver Cromwell. John West, in this second edition, reveals both notions to be misconceptions. In the remarkably succinct introduction, he demonstrates that the wars began not in England in 1642, but in 1639 as a conflict between Charles and his Scottish subjects which only later engulfed Ireland and then England and Wales. It is also a common misconception in gameshow questions as well as in other popular television programmes that Cromwell was the leader of parliament's forces from the outset. Yet by the middle of 1643, when the focus of this work is set, Cromwell was a colonel in command of a regiment of horse (cavalry) whose national image was in its infancy. Oliver Cromwell had been an inappropriate choice for military command when, during the previous summer, he had been given the rank of captain, very much as a political appointment. He was then 43 years old and had absolutely no military experience, even in the Trained Bands – the county-based militia. Nevertheless, he learned the trade remarkably quickly and had commanded a regiment since the beginning of 1643. During the spring he had demonstrated an ability to defeat royalist forces in small skirmishes and by July was trusted with *ad hoc* command of the horse regiments of the Eastern Association, parliament's grouping of East Anglian counties and a few East Midland shires. In July 1643 Cromwell was put under the command of Sir John Meldrum, a Scottish professional soldier in the service of parliament charged with relieving the siege of Gainsborough. It was in this capacity and role that Cromwell fought in the action described here.

As John West shows in his account of the first stage of the Battle of Gainsborough, Cromwell demonstrated both his developing mastery of the battlefield and tight command and control of his forces. Furthermore, when you read the letters selected for the appendix, you will see Cromwell was also developing his talent for the 17th century soundbite: he knew these letters would become public knowledge. Notice, too, how infrequently he mentions Sir John Meldrum in his description of the battle. Despite the somewhat ignominious end to the day's fighting, Cromwell was able to extract his forces successfully in the face of the enemy: by all accounts, the actions at Gainsborough were a crucially important point in Oliver Cromwell's career.

This is an excellent account of the siege and battle of Gainsborough and how it fits into the broader history of the town and the nation. The accompanying guide to Gainsborough's related historical sites provides an extremely useful aid to the visitor. The battlefield itself is one of the most accessible of the civil war battles, as it is in walking distance of the town centre. It is also just across the road from Gainsborough's Lea Road railway station. The plateau upon which the dramatic conflict took place is still accessible to those who can climb the steep hill to it. Even though houses are now built on the western slope of the hill, the visitor will still be impressed with the fact that Meldrum and Cromwell's men were able to fight their way up to the top in the face of stiff opposition. John West's account will be a necessary accompaniment to such a visit.

Professor Martyn Bennett
Nottingham Trent University

FOREWORD BY
KEVIN WINTER AND DON SMITH
OF THE BATTLEFIELD TRUST

WE WOULD like to thank John West for giving us the opportunity to write a foreword for this book. The Battlefields Trust is a registered charity dedicated to the protection, preservation and interpretation of Britain's battlefields. Founded in 1993, it is organised on a regional basis, with Gainsborough sitting in the East Midlands Region. Regular walks and talks are arranged for members and to attract non-members. Since 2017 Don Smith has been leading tours of Gainsborough battlefield close to the anniversary of the battle. Heritage England currently has 46 registered battlefields on their list and currently (2020) we are trying to add Gainsborough to that list, as it is under threat of development.

As you will discover from John's account, Gainsborough was not a major battle. However, its importance lies in the effects it had. Firstly by demonstrating Oliver Cromwell's military capabilities for the first time, as he showed his ability to take advantage of terrain, maintain control of his troops and deploy them aggressively when the opportunity arose.

These were the skills that would allow his success in subsequent actions at Winceby in October 1643, Marston Moor and Naseby. The abilities that Cromwell displayed for the first time at Gainsborough would see him rise from an obscure Huntingdonshire MP in 1642 to Lieutenant General of the New Model Army in 1645, when he was in command of the cavalry and second in command to Sir Thomas Fairfax overall. He led the campaign in Ireland in 1649 and took overall command of the New Model Army in 1650, against the Scots in the Third Civil War. He went on to become Lord Protector of England between 1653 and his death in 1658, and is the name that most people associate with the parliamentarian cause.

For the royalists, the effects were more immediate as they lost two senior commanders during the Gainsborough campaign. The death of Sir Robert Pierrepont, by friendly fire on 25 July, brought the loss of the second in command of royalist forces in Lincolnshire and East Anglia. A more severe loss was that of Charles Cavendish, who was only 23 years old. He had distinguished himself at Edgehill before being given command of the Duke of York's regiment. He was appointed Colonel General in command of royalist forces in Nottinghamshire and Lincolnshire. Basing himself at Newark, he had been involved in the capture of Grantham in March 1643 and the skirmish at Ancaster in April. He had escorted Queen Henrietta Maria's convoy from Newark on its way to Oxford, taking Burton-on-Trent on 2 July 1643. Following his death, he was buried in Newark before being reinterred with his family in Derby 30 years later. Much more would have been expected from such a young general and his loss would have been keenly felt by the royalists.

Find out more about the battle and the effects on Gainsborough as you read John's book.

To find out more about the Battlefields Trust visit:

www.battlefieldstrust.com

Kevin Winter:
Chair Battlefields Trust East Midlands

Don Smith:
Vice Chair Battlefields Trust East Midlands and Gainsborough Battlefield Guide

A BRIEF HISTORY OF THE ENGLISH CIVIL WAR

IN 1640 Charles I had been on the throne for 15 years. He was a stubborn and inflexible man who regarded his right to rule as a divine gift from God himself. He had frequently clashed with parliament, who wanted a larger say in how the nation was governed. Unpopular taxes and the belief that he was unduly influenced by his Catholic wife in matters of religion – England being a Protestant country – only made matters worse. In 1629 Charles dissolved parliament and decided to rule alone. This was later to become known as the 'Eleven Years Tyranny'. During these years he imposed unpopular taxes on the people such as the notorious 'ship money' in which all towns on the coast had to pay for the upkeep of the navy. This was later extended to cover inland areas including the whole

Chatles I

of Lincolnshire. In one year alone, Charles demanded £8,000 from the county. Many regarded the tax as illegal and this aroused even more widespread anger against the king.

Further resentment in Lincolnshire was generated by Charles's decision to drain the fens into farmland to provide extra funds for the royal purse. That the livelihoods of many depended on the fens remaining common land counted for little and his unpopularity soared.

During this period, Charles appointed a new Archbishop of Canterbury, William Laud, who wished to make the Anglican Church more ceremonial. Puritans accused Laud of trying to reintroduce Catholicism with the blessing of the king. In 1637 three opponents of Laud, John Bastwick, Henry Burton, and William Prynne, had their ears cut off for writing pamphlets attacking Laud's religious policies. This action shocked many and caused further resentment towards the king.

Charles's inept handing of church matters proved disastrous and his attempt to introduce the *Anglican Book of Common Prayer* into Scotland was the straw that finally broke the camel's back. Riots broke out in Edinburgh and the king decided to send troops to bring the Scots to heel. A poorly trained army marched to the border and several indecisive skirmishes were fought. Money was needed to continue the campaign and Charles was reluctantly forced to call a new parliament to raise funds.

Charles's hopes for a compliant House of Commons were soon dashed. Parliament used the opportunity to demand a redress of grievances, the

GVILLAVME ARCHEVESQVE
DE CANTORBERY ET PRIMAT DAMGLETTERRE
William Arch- B: of Canterbury Prymat of all England, etc..

Laud's religous policies played a part in England's drift into civil war.

abandonment of ship money, and a complete change in the ecclesiastical system. Charles angrily refused their demands and again dissolved them.

The war with Scotland went from bad to worse with the defeat of the royal army and the invasion of Northumberland and County Durham.

The king was forced to sign a humiliating treaty in which he had to pay for the daily maintenance of the Scottish army on English soil.

Troops from Charles's army at this time were quartered in and around Gainsborough and sadly proved less than disciplined. An assault on a gentle-maid near the town was just one of the crimes recorded as having been committed by his conscripted soldiers.

The king was again forced to call another parliament but found them even more determined to speak out against his autocratic rule. They attacked his record in government and demanded the impeachment of his chief advisers, Stafford and Laud. He reluctantly gave in and both men were later executed.

A rebellion in Ireland only made matters worse. In 1641 Irish Catholics had risen up against English Protestant settlers. Stories were circulated in England that terrible atrocities had been committed against the English, with thousands alleged murdered or maimed. Charles wished to raise funds for troops to restore order, but parliament feared that he might use the army against his enemies in England and so resisted his demands for money to crush the uprising.

Both sides were now heading for war and Charles's attempt, in January 1642, to arrest his six leading critics in parliament proved a disaster. He led an armed guard to parliament but found that the men had fled. No English sovereign had ever acted this way before and his invasion of the chamber was considered a breach of parliamentary privilege. In one fell

The Earl of Stafford was blamed by many for advising Charles to pursue unpopular policies.

swoop, Charles had destroyed all the efforts of his supporters to portray him as a man of moderation and good sense.

The king decided to leave London and head north. Tradition states that he passed through Gainsborough on his way to Nottingham where,

Charles raises the Royal Standard at Nottingham.

By the sword divided -Parliament and Crown meet in battle.

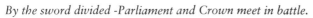

in August 1642, he raised the Royal Standard. By doing this and by summoning loyal subjects to join him, Charles declared war on parliament and lit the fuse of civil war. Inauspiciously for him, 'the standard itself was blown down the same night ... by a ... strong and unruly wind,' a contemporary account of the time recorded.

The next few years saw the entire nation ravaged by armed conflict as both sides sought to gain the upper hand in battle. In 1645 Charles was decisively defeated at Naseby by parliament's New Model Army. Despite this massive victory, he refused to give up hope and the war limped on for another year.

In May 1646 Charles sought shelter with the Presbyterian Scottish Army, who were stationed in Nottinghamshire. They agreed to hand

King Charles I at Naseby

Riding into battle.

him over to parliament in exchange for a large sum of money. The king was delivered to the parliamentary commissioners in January 1647, but negotiations between the two failed. He refused to accept a limit to his powers and behind parliament's back he negotiated with the Scots to back him militarily in exchange for introducing Presbyterianism into England

A battle of the English Civil War.

– a promise that Charles had no intention of keeping. The outbreak of the Second Civil War in 1648 finally convinced the army leaders and some sections of parliament that the king could not be trusted. After the

A battle scene from the English Civil War.

A fight to the death.

defeat of the royalist and Scottish armies, it was decided that Charles must be brought to account for all the bloodshed he had caused since 1642. In December 1648 parliament was purged by the army of all those MPs still wishing to find a peace compromise. The remainder, the Rump House of Commons, as it became known, moved to put the king on trial.

In January 1649, The Rump indicted Charles Stuart on a charge of treason. They declared themselves capable of legislating alone without

The trial of Charles I.

The execution of Charles I

the need of a sovereign and passed a bill creating a separate court for the trial.

The trial began on 20 January 1649, with Charles accused of using his power to pursue his interests over the good of the country. He was found guilty of treason and executed on 30 January 1649.

England was declared a republic for the first and only time in its history. The republic would last until 1660 when Charles's son was invited to return as Charles II.

GAINSBOROUGH AND THE CIVIL WAR

THE FIRST recorded reference to Gainsborough is to be found in the Anglo-Saxon Chronicle of 1013. However, it is safe to assume that the Celts and Romans would have found the fertile land to the east of the Trent suitable for habitation and farming. Following the collapse of Roman rule in the fifth century, Saxon immigrants began to move into the area and their first settlements would have consisted of small farms dotted along the river. The name Gainsborough probably derives from the Gaini tribe who were living in the area in the sixth century. In 868 King Alfred the Great married Ealswitha, daughter of Aethelred Mucill, chief of the Gaini.

As the Saxons gained supremacy over England, various kingdoms began to be established, with Gainsborough finding itself at a strategic crossing of the Trent, on the frontiers of Mercia and Northumbria. During the reign of Ethelred the Unready, Gainsborough was occupied by the Danish King Sweyn Forkbeard during his wars with the Saxons. Ethelred finally fled to Normandy and in 1013 Sweyn was declared king. He died in Gainsborough the following year and was succeeded by his

King Canute.

son Canute who later found fame for supposedly trying to command the tides to turn back. Some believe that this futile display of kingly power took place in Gainsborough and may have involved Canute attempting to influence the River Trent's aegir, a tidal bore.

The Domesday Book of 1086 records only 80 people living in Gainsborough. A large proportion were of Scandinavian descent. The decades following the Norman invasion of 1066 saw the town continue to grow and during the reign of King John it was granted a weekly market.

In 1322 Gainsborough was named as one of the ports supplying the king with corn, and by the 16th century it had replaced nearby Torksey as the main inland port of the area. The town also boasted a quarry, windmills and gypsum mine, which further aided its growth as a major centre of commerce and trade for the area.

By the 17th century Gainsborough was a successful port, trading and farming centre. Two annual fairs were held in the town and these attracted goods and merchants from as far away as London. In 1642 the town's population consisted of approximately 1,800 people, whose trades included merchants, butchers, leather workers, textile manufacturers, carpenters, plasterers, bakers, innkeepers and brewers. The town was triangular in shape and covered an area of about one and a quarter miles from north to south and a quarter of a mile from east to west. The centre lay around All Saints Church, the market and the Old Hall. The town lacked a bridge at this time and a ferry served as a crossing point for those wishing to travel across the river into Nottinghamshire.

Apart from the stone church and brick-and-timber hall, the remainder of Gainsborough would have consisted of timber-framed buildings which lined the main streets of Bridge Street (then known as Cawsey), Lord Street, Market Street (then called Beastmarket) and Silver Street. The latter acquired its name after Charles I decreed that the street's businesses should pay their annual rents in silver. The town also had a 'Free Grammar School' which had been founded by royal charter in 1589. The schoolmaster in 1642 was John Merryweather. He proved a less than able charge as in 1643 he is recorded as having fled the school at the approach of the royalist army. His pupils were left alone to play!

A large wood (now known as Warren Wood), to the south of the town, provided a ready supply of fresh rabbit meat and skins for the town's traders and inhabitants. This area is still full of rabbits to this day.

To the east lay a low line of hills with streams running off them. These, when in spate, often flooded the roads on the outskirts of the town. The area was used as arable land and was cultivated in strips by freeholders in the town. To the north and south lay meadows known as North Marsh and Humblecarr and were used to pasture animals.

When war was declared, Gainsborough lay in an area which was sympathetic to the parliamentary cause. Sir John Wray of Glentworth and Wharton, the Tywhitts of Scotter and Kettleby, Lord Willoughby of

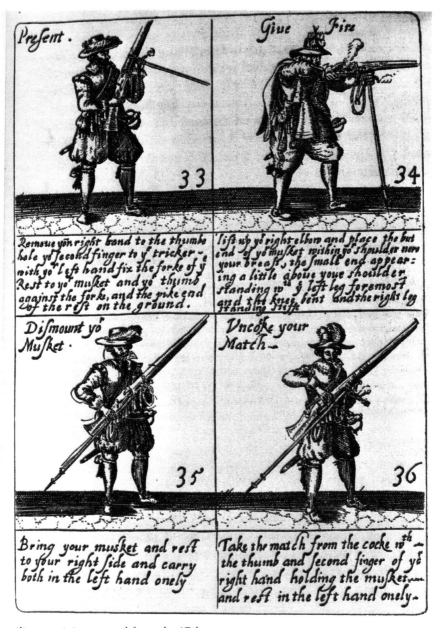

A military training manual from the 17th century.

Parham and Edmund Edward Rossiter of Somerby were all supporters of parliament and could be counted on to resist the king's demands. Sir Willoughby Hickman of The Old Hall in Gainsborough was also thought to be a supporter of parliament but was later accused of royalist sympathies in 1644 and fined. His son was later held suspect by parliament.

Royalist supporters in the area included Lord Jermyn of Torksey, Sir Thomas Williamson of East Markham and Gainsborough, Marmaduke Darcy of Knaith and George Lassels of Beckingham. Lord Jermyn had a house at Torksey that was attacked by parliamentary troops and burnt down. The ruins of his house can still be seen beside the Trent.

The town may have been divided in its sympathies but decided to remain neutral in the forlorn hope that both sides would leave them alone. The people of Gainsborough were not alone in wishing to remain neutral, and towns such as Worksop and Retford also attempted to stay out of the conflict.

Gainsborough was of strategic importance to both sides, situated on a crossing of the Trent as well as important roads leading both south and north. It was obvious that both sides would seek control of the town and in 1642 a committee was formed for its protection. Weapons were gathered and a company of '6 score men' was formed. A series of earth banks and ditches were dug to the south of the town as there was no natural defence in this area. These earthworks were still visible in the early 19th century. The river to the west, a drainage ditch to the north and boggy ground to the east were presumably considered enough defence with the result that no earthworks were erected in these areas.

Any hope that both sides would respect Gainborough's neutrality were dashed in March 1643 when Sir John Henderson sent out a raiding party from royalist held Newark. The town was surrounded early one morning with the demand that it be immediately surrendered. This was quickly done with not a shot being fired in the town's defence.

In March the Earl of Denbigh wrote to the Parliamentary Committee of Safety 'of the apprehensions and panic which, as the enemy reports, Lincoln and Gainsborough have in abandoning themselves to the mercy of the contrary party.'

Gainsborough was put under the command of the Earl of Kingston, who had recently declared his support for Charles. In May and June the garrison, together with troops from Newark, raided the surrounding area. Lincoln was attacked, where they clashed with the garrison. Parliament's Sir Edward Ayscough and John Broxholme wrote to parliament's Speaker Lenthall that 'the malignant party at Gainsborough, being assured that the strength of our horse was joined to the great body about Nottingham were puffed with such boldness as … to range over the country, to assess towns, to take prisoners and to drive men's horses.'

On 1 June Sir John Brook, Captain Whichcote and Sir Charles Dallison led a group of horse and dragoons to attack Market Rasen. Louth was attacked the following day and occupied. Parliament sent a force from Lincoln to drive them out, capturing 100 royalists in the process. On 1 July another royalist attack on Lincoln by troops from Gainsborough

Lincoln Cathedral at the time of the English Civil War.

and Newark was beaten off despite the attempts of Hotham, a senior parliamentary officer, to betray the city.

Matters came to a head when powder intended for parliamentary troops in Rotherham was seized at Gainsborough. Parliament decided to act and sent Lord Willoughby of Parham – appointed in 1643 by parliament as Lord-Lieutenant and Commander-in-Chief in Lincolnshire – to remove this thorn from their side. Willoughby arrived at Gainsborough on 20 July and seized the town before Kingston's troops could call to arms. Kingston retreated to his headquarters and was only taken prisoner after the house had been set on fire. The earl was taken under guard by the

The right Honourable the
Lord Willoughby of Parham etc -

river to Hull but the boat came under fire from royalist troops on the

riverbank and he was hit by a cannon ball, which cut him in half.

Willoughby's triumph at Gainsborough was to be short-lived. With the fall

of the town, the royalists had lost their communication link with Newark and

immediately sent a relieving force, a detachment of the Earl of Newcastle's

Charles Cavendish.

army, under the 23-year-old Sir Charles Cavendish, a cousin of the Earl. As Lord Willoughby exclaimed, 'the same day I tooke it I was beseaged before night, and there kept in some ten days before I had any release'.

Parliament wanted the town to be relieved and troops, under Sir John Meldrum from Nottingham and Colonel Oliver Cromwell

Sᵣ John Meldrum

from Cambridgeshire, were ordered to combine forces and attack Cavendish's besieging army. Cromwell had only recently captured a royalist stronghold at Burghley House and so rushed north to join Meldrum (at this point Oliver's commander as he had been given the task of leading regional forces in order to relieve Gainsborough), taking

Engraved by W. Sharp, from an original Picture in the possession of R. Dalton Esq.

London. Publish'd May 7th 1789, by T. Cadell, Strand.

Cromwell in the 1640s.

A Royalist cavalry charge.

with him 600 horse and dragoons. The two met up on 27 July at North

Scale, some ten miles south of Gainsborough, where they were joined

by a further detachment from Lincoln. At 2am the following day, a

force of 20 troops of horse and foot and three or four companies of

A Royalist falls in battle.

dragoons including detachments from Northamptonshire, some 1,200 men in all, headed north. Cromwell's troops brought up the rear.

At the village of Lea, about a mile and a half from the town, they met a 'forlorn hope' of a 100-royalist horse. This was engaged and, after a short skirmish, was driven back to Cavendish's main body, which had been drawn up to the immediate south of the town on the top of a hill. which later became known as Foxby Hill.

The royalists consisted of three regiments of horse and a reserve from Cavendish's horse. The parliamentarians were at a disadvantage as the slope was steep and littered with rabbit warrens. Despite this, Cromwell and Meldrum decided to attack. The Lincolners slowly advanced up the hill and soon found themselves face to face with the royalist cavalry who were, according to Cromwell, only a musket shot away. As they were forming up, the royalists attacked in the hope they could take them at a disadvantage. Cromwell, who was in command of the right wing, charged forward and, as he later said, 'came up horse to horse; where we disputed it with our swords and pistols a pretty time; all keeping close order, so that one could not break the other.'

The battle raged on, with Cromwell gradually gaining the advantage, forcing the royalist horse to fall back. This retreat soon became a rout with the royalists being chased by the parliamentary cavalry for some five or six miles. Meldrum then moved into Gainsborough with a force of 200 men and relieved Willoughby's beleaguered garrison.

But all was not yet lost for the royalists. Cavendish had kept a regiment in reserve and taking advantage of the fact that part of the parliamentary horse had left launched a counter-attack into the Lincolnshire troops

Pitting brother against brother and father against son. The English Civil War often divided families.

who had remained behind. They were thrown back and it appeared that Cavendish may yet win the day. But Cromwell had not left in pursuit of the royalist cavalry and had kept back Major Whalley and a reserve of three troops of horse.

Cromwell later described what happened next: 'Immediately I fell on his rear with my three troops; which did so astonish him, that he did give over the chase, and would fain have delivered himself from me. But I pressing on forced "them" down a hill, having good execution of them; and below the hill, drove the General with some of his soldiers into a quagmire ...'

Cavendish received an injury to the head and was knocked off his horse. A sword thrust in the chest by a Captain-General Berry proved fatal and he died in the town some two hours later. He was later taken to Newark for burial. The spot where he received his wounds was originally known as Black Sike, but by 1677 had been renamed Candish Bog.

There was nothing romantic about such battles and we can imagine dead and dying men and horses littering the hillside and surrounding fields. The names later given to the fields here, Graves Close and Redcoats Field, aptly describe the slaughter that took place here on that grim day in 1643.

With the battle over, Cromwell set about supplying Willoughby with supplies of food, powder and ammunition to help the town withstand a future siege. It was at this point that Cromwell was informed that a royalist force of six troops of horse and 300 foot was advancing on

William Cavendish, 1st duke of Newcastle.

Gainsborough from the north. Cromwell had no foot soldiers and so

Willoughby gave him 600 men from the Gainsborough garrison to deal

with what Cromwell assumed was a remnant of Cavendish's forces not

yet engaged. Cromwell and Meldrum rode north along the low ridge

45

Oliver Cromwell rides into battle.

of hills to the east of the town. As they neared the village of Morton, they encountered two troops of horse near a mill. These were engaged and driven back to the village. Cromwell's forces marched on and found themselves at the summit of a hill (probably Spital Hill), where they were shocked to see not a small royalist force but an entire army, who had crossed the Trent by using a bridge of boats further north. As Cromwell was to later to recall, 'We saw in the bottom, about a quarter of a mile from us, a regiment of foot; after that another; after that the Marquis of Newcastle's own regiment; consisting in all of about 50 foot colours, and a great body of horse, which indeed was Newcastle's Army. Which, coming so unexpectedly, put us to new consultations ...'

Willoughby's soldiers, upon seeing this great force, fell back in disorder to the town, but not before suffering causalities due to a group of royalist horse who managed to engage them in combat. Cromwell realised that it was suicide to take on Newcastle's army or retreat into the town. This, together with the fact that his men and horses were exhausted by the recent battle, made him order a withdrawal. This was at first hampered by several hedgerows and they fell back some half a mile in disorder until they came to the end of a lane at the far end of a field. Cromwell then ordered a brilliant manoeuvre, which military historians still cite as a classic example of cavalry tactics.

Two rearguard parties of horse consisting of four troops of Cromwell's regiment and four of the Lincoln troop were sent under Captain Ayscough and Major Whalley to stand firm and retire alternately to cover Cromwell's main force. On eight or nine occasions, a handful of men held back the royalists with the loss of only two until they reached the safety of Lincoln and the parliamentary garrison there. Cromwell was generous in his praise and wrote that it was, 'Equal to any of late times and the Honour of it must belong to Major Whalley and Captain Ayscough.'

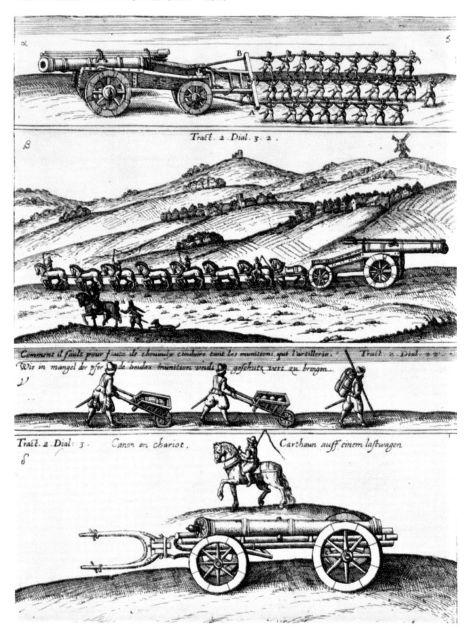

17th century siege cannon.

Cromwell's star was firmly in the ascendant after this battle and within ten years his enormous military and political achievements would make him the only choice to lead the nation as Lord Protector of a republican government.

Newcastle was now besieging Gainsborough and set up 16 pieces of ordnance and some mortars around the town. Willoughby refused to surrender and the order was given to fire upon the town. The siege lasted for three days, with the people there suffering great hardship as the continued bombardment caused fires to break out. The townsfolk started to harass Willoughby's soldiers and even threatened to surrender the town themselves. Willoughby, realising that a relief force would not arrive in time, was forced to ask for terms on 31 July. Newcastle's terms of surrender were that the officers could depart with their weapons but no common soldier should be allowed to leave the town in arms. He further stipulated that all royalist prisoners be released and that all colours, ordnance and ammunition be left behind, along with the keys of the town. The defeated parliamentarians were then allowed to leave for Lincoln, but not before some suffered ill-treatment at the hands of the recently liberated royalist garrison. Lincoln did not remain in their hands for long and Willoughby and his men were forced to abandon the city and retreat to Boston.

Cromwell wrote to parliament about the dangers of allowing Gainsborough to remain in the royalist's hands. Before its surrender, he had pleaded for a force of 2,000 men to be raised to relieve Willoughby to ensure that parliament's hold over Lincolnshire and beyond remained secure. 'You will see them [Newcastle's army] in the bowels of your Association [the Eastern counties],' he warned.

Newcastle did not remain in Gainsborough long and left to lay siege to the parliamentarian garrison in Hull. A subordinate, Colonel St George, remained in charge and used Gainsborough as a base for continued attacks on the areas held by parliament. He also set up defences at Burton-on-Stather to protect the river from the north. Lincoln was recaptured by parliament in October and a plot by Colonel St George to bribe an innkeeper named Towle to betray the city was foiled.

Those suspected or known to have Puritan leanings were made to feel distinctly uncomfortable during the royalist occupation, and some left the town. Matthew and William Kirk had supplied parliament with arms, horses and money and found themselves in prison. They were forced to pay £240 for their release and had all their goods seized.

Cromwell's former colleague, Sir John Meldrum, was given the task of retaking Gainsborough, and on 18 December 1643 he attacked. A small fleet of boats from Hull fired on the fort at Burton-on-Stather while Meldrum, with a body of horse, attacked it from the land. The fort fell and the combined force now pushed on to Gainsborough. The boats fired on the town and on 20 December the royalists surrendered, with over 600 prisoners, 500 arms and nine pieces of ordnance being taken.

Gainsborough was now occupied for the next four months, with Meldrum taxing the inhabitants in order to maintain the garrison there. The town was now used as a base to attack scattered pockets of royalist resistance in the Isle of Axholme and elsewhere. In February he

Edward Montague Earl of Manchefter.

attacked and captured a 'Royal Fort' (possibly at West Stockwith), together with five boats on the river that had been carrying provisions for Newcastle's army.

In March 1644 Meldrum evacuated the town and destroyed the defences due to the approach of royalist forces under Prince Rupert after a parliamentary attempt to take Newark had failed. Meldrum retreated to the safety of Hull. He later wrote that, 'if Gainsborough had not been raised by my order, the enemy might have found a nest to have hatched much more mischief at this time.'

This setback was short-lived and parliament was soon on the offensive again, with the Earl of Manchester marching into Lincolnshire with

A soldier of the English Civil War.

a fresh army. Lincoln was retaken and on 25 May 1644 Manchester crossed the Trent at Gainsborough using a bridge of boats. He was on his way to meet the royalist army at Marston Moor and fight a battle that would see Charles I suffer his greatest defeat in the war so far. After the battle, Manchester returned south and quartered part of his army in the town. Records show that Gainsborough was ordered to pay £80 towards the upkeep of the army by the Committee of Lincoln.

Soldiers continued to be quartered in the town to prevent further royalist attempts to retake it. This continued until at least 1646, as in February of that year a meeting was held in Gainsborough to deal with the complaints of civilians from Tickhill and elsewhere regarding the behaviour of some soldiers and officers of the Scots army.

By the end of 1646 it appeared that the war was at an end, with Charles defeated and held by parliament's allies, the Scottish Presbyterians. For the people of Gainsborough, it must have seemed like they had seen the end of the war and all its accompanying horrors, but their relief was to be short-lived.

In 1648 royalist uprisings in support of the still captive Charles I broke out across the country. In Lincolnshire, support for the uprisings was distinctly frosty and few flocked to the king's cause. On 23 June royalists from Doncaster, some 400 horse and 200 musketeers, moved on the Isle of Axeholme. On the morning of 30 June they reached the Trent and crossed over to Gainsborough by ferry. The town was not garrisoned and so could offer no resistance as the royalists moved on to take Lincoln. The city fell and arms and money were seized and sent back to Gainsborough. Parliament responded quickly to this new crisis, with Sir Henry Cholmeley marching on the town and forcing the royalists to fall back across the Trent. The final clash came at Willoughby near Nottingham with the royalists defeated. The Second Civil War, as it later became known, was over.

Gainsborough had suffered badly during the Civil War due to its strategic position, having made it a valuable prize for both sides. Many buildings were damaged or destroyed but, despite this destruction, it is surprising to discover that only a few civilians are recorded as having been killed during the fighting. The town also suffered financially as the inhabitants were forced to pay taxes to maintain the troops quartered there. Trade and industry also declined due to the disruption of commerce, but some traders ironically benefitted from the war by supplying equipment to the garrison; Parish records of the time refer to spur makers and sword dressers in the town.

Royalist sympathisers in the town now faced punishment in the wake of parliament's victory. Sir Willoughby Hickham of The Old Hall was fined. Edward Nicholson lost one-sixth of his estates and Peter Dickinson was fined £110 for being a member of the royalist garrison at Newark. This was later reduced to £80 as he 'had but a small estate and is so much indebted'. Another royalist, Caesar Sanderson, lost one-sixth of his estate.

OLIVIER CROMWELL, General des Armées de la Republique Angloise, Lieutenant et Gouuerneur d'Irlande, & Chancelier de l'Académie d'Oxford.

B. Moncornet excudit Auec priuilege du Roy

Oliver Cromwell in the early 1650s.

In 1649 Charles I was executed and Britain was made a republic, a Commonwealth, governed by parliament and then, in 1653, by Oliver Cromwell as Lord Protector.

During the Protectorate coins were struck bearing the image of Cromwell as Lord Protector.

A garrison continued to be maintained in Gainsborough in the 1650s as Colonel Overton, Governor of Hull, wrote of hoping to obtain seaman for the republican navy from the garrisons of York, Whitby, Selby, Bridlington, Scarborough and Gainsborough. Abortive royalist uprisings of 1655 did not affect the town, and life continued as much as it had done before the Civil War, with houses rebuilt and trade and commerce finally returning to normal.

Cromwell died in 1658 and was succeeded by his son, Richard. His accession was generally greeted with approval

The death mask of Oliver Cromwell.

Cromwell's wax effigy at Somerset House. The public lying in state began on 18 October and lasted until 10 November 1658.

in Lincolnshire. A paper of the time, the *Mercurius Politicus*, records that he was hailed by 6,000 Lincolnshire men as succeeding to a 'peaceable and prosperous government'. Sadly, Richard proved to be nothing like his father and was ousted after just a few months by disgruntled army officers. The republic began to fall apart as rival factions sought to take power for themselves or for the exiled Charles Stuart. Royalist agents became active again and in 1659 the republican Council of State in London wrote to Captain Cust in Lincoln to thank him for seizing arms at Gainsborough and to request that he question suspected royalists, a 'Mr Neville's steward, the carpenter Jones, and the carrier'.

Richard Cromwell succeded his father as Lord Protector in September 1658. He was forced to resign in May 1659.

In 1660 the republic collapsed and Charles was invited to return to Britain as king. What the people of Gainsborough thought about this turn of events is sadly not recorded, although one can imagine a general feeling of relief in the town that another armed conflict had been avoided.

Several former members of Cromwell's army are recorded as living in the area in the 1660s. One, a Mr Norton, was accused of telling another 'that honest men and old officers about Gainsborough' were ready to rise against the king. A nonconformist sect, the Anabaptists, held meetings in the town and one member, Jeremy Marsden, was named by authorities in 1663 as attempting to overthrow the royalist government in one of several abortive plots hatched in the 1660s.

The decades following the restoration of the monarchy would see Gainsborough settle down to a long period of peace, growth and prosperity. The town would not find itself under attack again until Hitler's Luftwaffe bombed it in World War Two.

PLACES OF CIVIL WAR INTEREST IN GAINSBOROUGH

THE BATTLEFIELD, FOXBY HILL

THE DECADES following the Civil War saw the town expand and gradually encroach upon the fringes of the battle. Today, the main battlefield on Foxby Hill, overlooking Lea Road, is still relatively free from development and remains much as it did in the 17th century. Climbing Foxby Hill will bring you to a clearing on the right of the road. Here can be found a stone monument to the battle, erected by Gainsborough Town Council in 1995. The plaque reads:

THE BATTLE OF GAINSBOROUGH 28 JULY 1643

IN THIS BATTLE OF THE ENGLISH CIVIL WAR
PARLIAMENTARY TROOPS LED BY OLIVER CROMWELL
ENGAGED AND DEFEATED CHARLES 1ST ROYALIST ARMY
ON OPEN GROUND TO THE EAST OF THE TOWN

(John West)

THIS MONUMENT ERECTED BY

GAINSBOROUGH TOWN COUNCIL WAS UNVEILED BY

DR PETER GAUNT

CHAIRMAN THE CROMWELL ASSOCIATION

ON 28 JULY 1995

(John West)

Walking further up the hill will take you to a small footpath that lies on the south side of the road. This leads to open fields and meadows

(John West)

(John West)

and the main area of the battlefield where Cromwell and Meldrum met Cavendish's forces. Lead musket balls dating from the 17th century have been found in this area.

The remnants of Warren Wood can be seen to the south. Candish Bog, where part of the royalist army and their leader fled after being defeated, lies to the west. The spot, now drained, where Cavendish was struck down by Captain-Lieutenant Barry has long since vanished under modern mill buildings.

To the north, another remnant of the royalist forces retreated in disorder towards the town. This area is now waste ground, playing fields and modern houses.

(John West)

Sadly, several of Gainsborough's 17th century buildings were demolished in the years following World War Two, a decision that many in the town now bitterly regret.

A blue plaque has been erected by The Delvers, a local history group, to commemorate the site of the Old Pillared House, which local tradition states was built on the site of a house used in 1643 by the royalists as their headquarters. It can be seen on the side of a Victorian building on Riverside Walk.

THE OLD HALL, PARNELL STREET, DN21 2NB

THE OLD Hall lies in the centre of the town and looks much as it did when the Civil War was being fought. Indeed, the building is now considered one of the best-preserved medieval manor houses in the whole of England.

The building was probably built in the 1460s (analysis of the roof timbers in the Great Hall shows that they were felled in that decade) by Sir Thomas Burgh, a prominent figure in local and national politics. As Lord of the Manor, money from the port and his tenants provided a healthy income but Sir Thomas also proved a generous benefactor and founded the Chantry and Alms House in the town.

In 1470 the hall was attacked by Sir Robert Welles, the 8th Baron Willoughby de Eresby, over disagreements about lands, status, and honour, but was not badly damaged.

On 10 October 1483 Richard III stayed one night at the hall during his journey from London to York. Sir Thomas held offices under Richard but changed sides

King Richard III.

Henry VIII is recorded as having visited the Old Hall in 1541.

and declared his support for Henry Tudor. After gaining the throne, a grateful Henry confirmed Thomas as Knight of the Body and Privy Councillor.

In August 1541, Henry VIII stayed there for three days with his wife, Catherine Howard. She was later accused of 'indiscretions' during her

Catherine Howard, the fifth wife of Henry VIII, was accused of indiscretions during her stay at the Old Hall.

time in Gainsborough. She would ultimately face the executioner's axe for this and other alleged extramarital affairs.

In 1510 Sir Thomas's son, Edward, was declared a lunatic and was incarcerated in the building. He died in 1528.

In 1596 the Burgh family fell on hard times and were forced to sell their home to William Hickman, a London merchant. William and his mother, Rose, were puritans and were sympathetic to the Separatists, Protestants who wished to separate from the perceived corruption of the Church of England and form independent local churches. The Hickmans allowed Separatist meetings to be held in the hall under the guidance of John Smyth, a local preacher. In 1620 a group of these Separatists, 'the

16th century bay window within the Great Hall (Figgis-West).

Pilgrim Fathers', sailed to America to escape religious persecution under James I.

Sir William may have been sympathetic to those who shared his religious persuasion, but he was less than sympathetic to the general townsfolk of Gainsborough. He enclosed part of the common field, had stalls demolished in the market square, levied tolls on corn passing through the town on the river and used money intended for the maintenance of the streets for his own use. He also declined to pay for the upkeep of the church and encouraged merchants from London to trade in Gainsborough, which resulted in the town's merchants being undersold.

At the outbreak of the Civil War, the head of the family was Sir Willoughby Hickman. He was related to some of the most prominent Puritan families in Lincolnshire and was the nephew of Lord Willoughby of Parham, the man who was later to attack and occupy the town in 1643. Hickman became a commissioner for raising parliamentary funds

Gainsborough Old Hall from the air.

and was also a member of the Sequestration Committee that dealt with confiscating the estates of the royalists who had fought against parliament. In November 1643, during the second royalist occupation of the town, Hickman accepted a baronetcy from Charles I. Despite protests to the contrary, he was now regarded as suspect and found himself fined £1,000 by parliament. This was later reduced to £50 due to the fact that his income derived from market tolls and other dependent estates.

Hickman died in 1650. His son, William, took over the estates. He had been a royalist supporter, but by 1653 he was trusted enough to be appointed High Sheriff of Nottingham. Despite this, he allowed secret royalist meetings to be held at the hall during Cromwell's rule as Lord Protector. With the return of Charles II in 1660, he was rewarded for his royalist sympathies with crown offices and the parliamentary seat of East Retford.

The Hickmans left the Hall in 1720. Although remaining in the family, it was leased for a variety of purposes including a theatre, linen factory, soup kitchen, masonic lodge, tenement housing, corn exchange, auction house and even a public house known as 'The Queen Adelaide'.

John Wesley, the founder of the Methodist Church, preached at the hall several times in the 1760s. He was less than impressed on his first visit and complained of 'a rude, wild multitude (a few of the better spirit excepted)'. However, he did concede that 'Yet all but 2 or 3 gentlemen were attentive while I enforced our Lord's words'.

The Great Hall (Figgis-West).

The building was given to the nation in the 1970s by the Bacon family, descendants of the Hickmans, and is now owned by English Heritage. It has many interesting features including a medieval kitchen, great dining hall, rooms displaying furniture from the 17th century and a Tudor brick tower. A climb to the top of the tower is well worth the effort as you will be rewarded by wonderful views of the town, river and surrounding countryside.

As with many old buildings, the Old Hall is said to be haunted. One ghost, the Grey Lady, apparently dates from the Tudor period when Elizabeth Burgh supposedly fell in love with a member of the Talbot family, who was a soldier by trade. Her father, Sir Thomas, refused her permission to marry below 'her station' with the result that the poor

The tower of the Old Hall (John West).

girl shut herself away in the tower bedroom where she died of a broken heart. A variation of the legend claims that she fell in love with a farmer and that her father locked her in the tower after she tried to elope and deliberately starved her to death.

Gainsborough Old Hall (Figgis-West).

The Great Hall (John West).

The haunted corridoor (Figgis-West).

In the early 1800s a man employed to paint the hall saw a lady dressed in white who was smiling at him. She beckoned him to follow her through a wall and became angry when he declined to do so. He collapsed in terror and was found repeating the words, 'She is there!'

In the 1940s several workmen were making repairs to the fabric of the hall when they saw a person in Tudor dress walk past them. They only realised that she was a ghost when the figure walked through a wall at the end of the corridor where they had been working. A search of the area where the figure had disappeared revealed a blocked-up doorway. She is also said to haunt the tower where she died. The sounds of footsteps and a closing door have been heard in this area, and in the 1990s I can remember speaking to one of the guides at the hall who told me that she had once seen 'a shadowy figure' standing by the stairway which leads to the tower roof.

Another ghost is that of a small boy, dressed in Victorian clothes, who has been seen in the West Wing, and a cavalier is also said to haunt the rooms and corridors and strange lights have been seen in the gift shop. Catherine Howard, Henry VIII's ill-fated wife, is rumoured to haunt the same area of the hall as the Grey Lady. A far older ghost is that of King Sweyn Forkbeard of Denmark. Legend claims that he died attacking a castle which stood on the site of the hall. His groans have supposedly been heard throughout the building. But one has to wonder how disembodied cries can be attributed to one particular ghost.

King Sweyn's ghost is supposed to haunt the Old Hall

The Old Hall is now owned by English Heritage. See the English Heritage website for entry prices and opening times. There is also a cafe and gift shop.

ALL SAINTS CHURCH, CHURCH STREET, DN21 2JS

THE FIRST mention of a church on this site dates from 1185 when Roger de Talbot, Lord of the Manor of Gainsborough, gave it to the Knights Templar of Willoughton in Lincolnshire. All that remains from the Civil War period is the imposing 15th century tower, some 90ft high, which houses eight bells dating from 1764 and 1856. It is constructed in the architectural style known as Perpendicular and includes a battlemented crown and imposing traceried windows.

The vicar during the Civil War was Robert Powell and he appears to have easily adapted to the changes brought about by the conflict and continued to hold his office throughout the Civil War, Cromwell's Protectorate and the return of the monarchy. That he was well regarded in the town is illustrated by the fact that in 1654 the pavement outside the vicarage was repaired at the town's expense 'out of Courtesie and respects' to him.

All Saints Church (Figgis-West).

The parish register for 1643 and 1644 records the burial in the churchyard of several soldiers and civilians killed during the fighting.

After the return of Charles II in 1660, several Puritans in the town refused to attend Anglican services in the church and were regularly ex-communicated by the church authorities.

The church had been allowed to deteriorate after the Civil War, and by the 18th century the building was being described by the church committee as being 'in a very ruinous and dangerous condition ... not capable of standing for any time, but on the contrary in imminent danger of falling'. An Act of Parliament authorised the demolition of the main body of the church, and loans, parish assessments and revenue raised through a duty on coal landed at Gainsborough paid for the new work. Demolition started in 1736 and it was not until 1744 that the church was again ready for worship. Further work on the building continued until October 1748.

Some were unhappy with the 'marrying' of the Gothic tower with the new building. A rhyme from the time records:

Gainsborough proud people,
Built a new church to an old steeple.

The interior of the church has been described by many as one of the finest examples of Georgian church architecture in England. The architect was Francis Smith, designer of All Saints in Derby, and features a central aisle,

The tower of All Saints Church (John West).

flanked by box pews, which leads to an apse at the east end. The roof and upper wooden balconies are supported by several fine Corinthian columns.

The interior of All Saints Church (Figgis-West)

All Saints Church (John West).

In 1903 vestries were built on either side of the tower, constructed in the Gothic style. The churchyard was cleared of its monuments and memorials in the 1950s.

In 1916 James Edward Standen, the vicar of Gainsborough, was sent a French document by Henry de Folleney who was the editor of the *Gazette Officielle de Guernsey*. It records a strange event which supposedly took place in the church in 1819.

'On Sunday, 4 April, 1819, summoned by the unusual ringing of the bells, three parishioners and Mr King, a minister, entered the church to find out what was happening. They anticipated something irregular and strange. Prayers were said before opening the door and again in the church. Then the brave group mounted the tower. There they saw

a seven-year-old child dressed in white and wearing a golden crown. He was ringing the bells simply by breathing on them. In answer to a challenge the child declared that he had been sent by God to call men to repentance, and he prophesied future trouble. 'Calamitous times are to come once more, forasmuch as men are showing themselves Godless, irreligious, and ungrateful throughout Europe; and this chiefly in such countries where Virtue and Truth ought to play the most shining part. For a long time God has awaited the fruits of justice but has found only the results of malice. So the Lord of Heaven has said: "In my anger I will scourge the Christian nations and punish them because of their wickedness ..." The King of France will do his utmost to extend his power. Great war preparations will be made throughout Europe. But the King of France's power shall be reduced by discord disturbing his kingdom and destroying it.' Then the boy led them into the church and commanded them to lift a stone. They tried without success, whereupon the child, chiding them for their lack of faith, turned it upside down and from underneath pulled out a scroll having 'England, England, renounce your wickedness. Make haste and repent' written on it in gold letters. The child then disappeared to more music, leaving the witnesses in ecstasy.'

The church is open daily.

GAINSBOROUGH HERITAGE CENTRE, 12 NORTH STREET, DN21 2HS

THE CENTRE, housed in the town's former post office and telephone exchange, contains exhibits and archive material relating to the history of the town. There is also a tea room and gift shop.

The centre is open three days a week, every Tuesday and Saturday 10am to 4pm and every Sunday 11am to 4pm.

You can join the Gainsborough Heritage Association by becoming a member for only £15 a year.

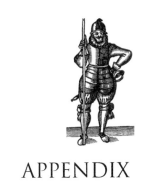

APPENDIX

Oliver Cromwell's letter on the Battle

To the Committee of the Association sitting at Cambridge. Huntingdon, 31 July, 1643.

GENTLEMEN, It hath pleased the Lord to give your servant and soldiers a notable victory now at Gainsborough. I marched after the taking of Burleigh House upon Wednesday to Grantham, where I met about 300 horse and dragooners of Nottingham. With these, by agreement, we met the Lincolners at North Scarle, which is about ten miles from Gainsborough, upon Thursday in the evening; where we tarried until two of the clock in the morning; and then with our whole body advanced towards Gainsborough.

About a mile and a half from the Town, we met a forlorn-hope of the enemy of near 100 horse. Our dragooners laboured to beat them back; but not alighting off their horses, the enemy charged them, and made them retire unto the main body. We advanced, and came to the bottom of a steep hill: we could not well get up but by some tracks; which our men essaying to do, the body of the enemy endeavoured to hinder; wherein we prevailed, and got the top of the hill. This was done by the Lincolners, who had the vanguard.

When we all recovered the top of the hill, we saw a great body of the enemy's horse facing us, at about a musket-shot or less distance; and a good Reserve of a full regiment of horse behind it. We endeavoured to put our men into as good order as we could. The enemy in the mean time advanced towards us, to take us at disadvantage; but in such order as we were, we charged their great body, I having the right wing; we came up horse to horse; where we disputed it with our swords and pistols a pretty time; all keeping close order, so that one could not break the other. At last, they a little shrinking, our men perceiving it, pressed in upon them, and immediately routed this whole body; some flying on one side and others on the other of the enemy's Reserve; and our men, pursuing them, had chase and execution about five or six miles.

I perceiving this body which was the Reserve standing still unbroken, kept back my Major, Whalley, from the chase; and with my own troop and the other of my regiment, in all being three troops, we got into a body. In this Reserve stood General Cavendish; who one while faced me, another while faced four of the Lincoln troops, which was all of ours that stood upon the place, the rest being engaged in the chase. At last General Cavendish charged the Lincolners, and routed them. Immediately I fell on his rear with my three troops; which did so astonish him, that he did give over the chase, and would fain have delivered himself from me. But I pressing on forced 'them' down a hill, having good execution of them; and below the hill, drove the General with some of his soldiers into a quagmire; where my Captain-lieutenant slew him with a thrust under his short ribs. The rest of the body was wholly routed, not one man staying upon the place.

After the defeat which was so total, we relieved the Town with such powder and provision as we brought with us. We had notice that there were six troops of horse and 300 foot on the other side of the Town, about a mile off us: we desired some foot of my Lord Willoughby's, about 400; and, with our horse and these foot, marched towards them: when we came towards the place where their horse stood, we went back with my troops to follow two or three troops of the enemy's who retired into a small village at the bottom of the hill. When we recovered the hill, we saw in the bottom, about a quarter of a mile from us, a regiment of foot; after that another; after that the Marquis of Newcastle's own regiment; consisting in all of about 50 foot colours, and a great body of horse; which indeed was Newcastle's Army. Which, coming so unexpectedly, put us to new consultations. My Lord Willoughby and I, being in the Town, agreed to call off our foot. I went to bring them off: but before I returned, divers of the foot were engaged; the enemy advancing with his whole body. Our foot retreated in disorder; and with some loss got the Town; where now they are. Our horse also came off with some trouble; being wearied with the long fight, and their horses tired; yet faced the enemy's fresh horse, and by several removes got off without the loss of one man; the enemy following the rear with a great body.

The honour of this retreat is due to God, as also all the rest: Major Whalley did in this carry himself with all gallantry becoming a gentleman and a Christian. Thus you have this true relation, as short as I could. What you are to

*do upon it, is next to be considered. The Lord direct you
what to do.*

Gentlemen,

I am Your faithful servant,

OLIVER CROMWELL.

Letter from Francis Willoughby to Oliver Cromwell.

To my noble Friend Colonel Cromwell at Huntingdon: These.

Boston, 5th August, 1643.

NOBLE SIR, Since the business of Gainsborough, the hearts of our men have been so deaded that we have lost most of them by running away. So that we were forced to leave Lincoln upon a sudden: and if I had not done it then, I should have been left alone in it. So that now I am at Boston; where we are very poor in strength; so that without some speedy supply, I fear we shall not hold this long neither.

My Lord General, I perceive, hath writ to you, To draw all the forces together. I should be glad to see it; for if that will not be, there can be no good to be expected. If you will endeavour to stop my Lord of Newcastle, you must presently draw them to him and fight him! For without we be masters of the field we shall be pulled out by the ears, one after another.

The foot, if they will come on, may march very securely

to Boston; which, to me, will be very considerable to your

Association. For if the Enemy get that Town, which is now

very weak for defence for want of men I believe they will

not be long out of Norfolk and Suffolk.

I can say no more: but desire you to hasten; and rest,

Your servant,

FRANCIS WILLOUGHBY

Willoughby was later to be accused by Cromwell and others of military incompetence and for allowing 'loose and profane' behaviour in his ranks. In early 1648 he travelled to the continent to join exiled royalists in plotting against his former colleagues.

More letters from Oliver Cromwell relating to events in Lincolnshire
Cromwell complains of Lord Grey's failure to join forces with him at
Stamford.

To the Honourable the Committee at Lincoln: These.

Lincolnshire, 3rd May, 1643.

*MY LORDS AND GENTLEMEN, I must needs be
hardly thought on; because I am still the messenger of
unhappy tidings and delays concerning you – though I
know my heart is to assist you with all expedition!*

*My Lord Grey hath now again failed me of the
rendezvous at Stamford, notwithstanding that both he
and I received Letters from his Excellency, commanding
us both to meet, and, together with Sir John Gell and the
Nottingham forces, to join with you. My Lord Grey sent
Sir Edward Hartop to me, To let me know he could not
meet me at Stamford according to our agreement; fearing
the exposing of Leicester to the forces of Mr. Hastings
and some other Troops drawing that way.*

*Believe it, it were better, in my poor opinion, Leicester
were not, than that there should not be found an*

immediate taking of the field by our forces to accomplish the common ends. Wherein I shall deal as freely with him, when I meet him, as you can desire. I perceive Ashby-de-la-Zouch sticks much with him. I have offered him now another place of meeting; to come to which I suppose he will not deny me; and that to be tomorrow. If you shall therefore think fit to send one over unto us to be with us at night – you do not know how far we may prevail with him: To draw speedily to a head, with Sir John Gell and the other forces, where we may all meet at a general rendezvous, to the end you know of. And then you shall receive full satisfaction concerning my integrity; and if no man shall help you, yet will not I be wanting to do my duty, God assisting me.

If we could unite those forces 'of theirs'; and with them speedily make Grantham the general rendezvous, both of yours and ours, I think it would do well. I shall bend my endeavours that way. Your concurrence by some able instrument to solicit this, might probably exceedingly hasten it; especially having so good a foundation to work upon as my Lord General's commands. Our Norfolk forces, which will not prove so many as you may imagine by six or seven hundred men, will lie conveniently at Spalding; and, I am confident, be ready to meet at Grantham at the general rendezvous.

I have no more to trouble you; but begging of God to take away the impediments that hinder our conjunction, and to prosper our designs, take leave.

Your faithful servant,

OLIVER CROMWELL

Oliver Cromwell on the Battle of Grantham.

To----: These.

Grantham, 13th May, 1643.

SIR, God hath given us, this evening, a glorious victory over our enemies. They were, as we are informed, one-and-twenty colours of horse-troops, and three or four of dragoons.

It was late in the evening when we drew out; they came and faced us within two miles of the town. So soon as we had the alarm, we drew out our forces, consisting of about twelve troops,whereof some of them so poor and broken, that you shall seldom see worse; with this handful it pleased God to cast the scale. For after we had stood a little, above musket-shot the one body from the other; and the dragooners had fired on both sides, for the space of half an hour or more; they not advancing towards us, we agreed to charge them. And, advancing the body after many shots on both sides, we came on with our troops a pretty round trot; they standing firm to receive us; and our men charging fiercely upon them, by God's providence they were immediately routed, and ran all away, and we had the execution of them two or three miles.

I believe some of our soldiers did kill two or three men apiece in the pursuit; but what the number of dead is we are not certain. We took forty-five Prisoners, besides divers of their horse and arms, and rescued many Prisoners, whom they had lately taken of ours: and we took four or five of their colours. I rest.

OLIVER CROMWELL

Cromwell asks for money and supplies.

To the Mayor, &c. of Colchester: These,

Lincolnshire, 28th May, 1643.

GENTLEMEN,

I thought it my duty once more to write unto you For more strength to be speedily sent unto us, for this great Service.

I suppose you hear of the great Defeat given by my Lord Fairfax to the Newcastle Forces at Wakefield. It was a great mercy of God to us. And had it not been bestowed upon us at this very present, my Lord Fairfax had not known how to have subsisted. We assure you, should the Force we have miscarry, expect nothing but a speedy march of the Enemy up unto you.

Why you should not strengthen us to make us subsist, judge you the danger of the neglect; and how inconvenient this improvidence, or unthrift, may be to you! I shall never write but according to my judgment: I tell you again, It concerns you exceedingly to be persuaded by me. My Lord Newcastle is near six-thousand foot, and above Sixty troops of horse; my Lord Fairfax is about Three-thousand foot, and Nine troops of horse; and we have about Twenty-four troops of horse and dragooners. The Enemy draws more to the Lord Fairfax: our motion and yours must be exceeding speedy, or else it will do you no good at all.

If you send, let your men come to Boston. I beseech you hasten the supply to us: forget not money! I press not hard; though I do so need, that, I assure you, the foot and dragooners are ready to mutiny. Lay not too much upon the back of a poor gentleman, who desires, without much noise, to lay down his life, and bleed the last drop to serve the Cause and you. I ask not your money for myself: if that were my end and hope, viz. the pay of my place, I would not open my mouth at this time. I desire to deny myself; but others will not be satisfied. I beseech you hasten supplies. Forget not your prayers.

Gentlemen, I am Yours,

OLIVER CROMWELL

Cromwell demands more soldiers.

For my noble Friends the Committee of the Association sitting: at Cambridge: These.

Huntingdon, 6th August, 1643.

GENTLEMEN,

You see by this Enclosed how sadly your affairs stand. It's no longer Disputing, but Out instantly all you can! Raise all your Bands; send them to Huntingdon;-get up what Volunteers you can; hasten your Horses.

Send these Letters to Norfolk, Suffolk and Essex, without delay. I beseech you spare not, but the expeditious and industrious! Almost all our Foot have quitted Stamford: there is nothing to interrupt an Enemy, but our Horse, that is considerable. You must act lively; do it without distraction. Neglect no means! I am

Your faithful servant,
OLIVER CROMWELL

Cromwell writes of discontent among his soldiers regarding lack of pay.

Boston, 11th September, 1643.

SIR,

Of all men I should not trouble you with money matters, did not the heavy necessities my Troops are in, press upon me beyond measure. I am neglected exceedingly!

I am now ready for my march towards the Enemy; who hath entrenched himself over against Hull, my Lord Newcastle having besieged the Town. Many of my Lord of Manchester's Troops are come to me: very bad and mutinous, not to be confined in ; they paid to a week almost; mine noways provided – for to support them, except by the poor Sequestrations of the County of Huntingdon! My Troops increase. I have a lovely company; you would respect them, did you know them. No 'Anabaptists'; they are honest sober Christians: they expect to be used as men!

If I took pleasure to write to the House in bitterness, I have occasion. 'Of' the 3,000l. allotted me, I cannot get the Norfolk part nor the Hertfordshire: it was given 'away' before I had it. I have minded your service to forgetfulness of my own Soldiers' necessities. I desire not to seek myself: 'but' I have little money of my own to help my Soldiers. My estate is little. I tell you, the Business of Ireland and England hath had of me, in money, between Eleven and Twelve Hundred pounds;-therefore my Private can do little to help the Public. You have had my money: I hope in God I desire to venture my skin. So do mine. Lay weight upon their patience; but break it not! Think of that which may be a real help. I believe 5,000l. is due.

If you lay aside the thought of me and my Letter, I expect no help. Pray for.

Your true friend and servant, OLIVER CROMWELL

William Sykes of Hull petitions the Lords for compensation after suffering financial hardship due to his support of the parliamentary cause. Sykes had been captured by the royalists at Gainsborough in 1643 and had suffered ill-treatment at their hands.

To the right honourable the Lords assembled in Parliament

The humble petition of William Sykes of Hull marchant

Sheweth that the petitioner out of his abundant and large affection to the Parliament the effects whereof he is able to prove by the testemony of divers worthy gentlemen of his owne contry who can sufficiently testifie his continual readynes upon all occasions for that honourable service wherein a verry great and large summe partly in arms and amunition of severall kinds mony and plate amountinge to the summe of eight thousand foure hundred sixtie three pounds eighteene shillinges five pence which is your petitioner whole estate may be an undoubted witnes besides the consideration mony amountinge to the vallue of two thousand five hundred elleven pondes foure shillings one penny both which said sommes by a perticular hereunto anexed may apeare

That your petitioner also haveinge no command layed upon him yet out of his abundant desire to advance the Parliamentes sarvice beinge then in a verry low condition did volluntarily adventure his parson and went from Hull to Gainsbrough in a sarvice which at that time did exceedingly concerne the northerne parts and was in that assault taken prissoner stript naked and exeedingly endangered

That he hath beene severall times plundred and taken prissoner by the enemy when he lived out of Hull and which adds more still to his forementioned losses his father dureinge his absence accasioned by these severall services did for his good affection to the Parliament alter his will and gave a way from him to his brothers which he intended to this petitioner to the vallue of thre hundred pondes per annum

He therefore most humbly prayes that this honourable house will be pleased to commisserate the estate of your poore petitioner as also to assigne him somme competent some for his present necessity and reliefe for his poore wife and children and the residue of his debt out of such delinquents estates as to your honores shall seeme expedient

And your petitioner shall ever pray etc

William Sykes

This petition was sent to the Lords in 1647. Sykes was a merchant in Hull who had served Parliament at Gainsborough. As already stated, he had been taken prisoner in the town by the royalists and had suffered abuse at their hands.

He had supplied Parliament with money, arms, ammunition and plate to the value of £8,463 18s 5d which, he claimed, attracted 'consideration money' (interest due as a 'reward') of £2,511 4s 1d. He further stated that because of his support for Parliament, his father had changed his will in his brothers' favour costing him £300 a year.

On 2 March 1647 the House of Lords ordered that the House of Commons should be 'specially recommended' to provide him with relief. On 22 April the House of Commons agreed in principle to pay William £4,000 plus interest at 8 per cent per annum. Despite this, the matter dragged on. On 11 May the Committee for Compounding issued the necessary warrant and although the Commons, the Lords and the Committee for Compounding had all agreed the payment, the Committee for Taking the Accounts had still not finished its work.

On 26 June Lord Willoughby (who had led the surprise attack on Gainsborough in 1643) wrote to the Chairman of the Committee supporting his claim. He confirmed William's efforts on behalf of Parliament, observing that 'he has suffered much for his good affection'. He urged the Committee to 'expedite his business under your hand'.

By December 1647 the money had still not been paid. The petition was then passed back and forth between committees with no tangible result. What Sykes thought of these constant delays is sadly not recorded.

On 10 June 1648 the Lords were advised that Sykes had been arrested 'and laid in prison' for his debts. The Lords again asked the Commons to take action.

On 31 July the matter was returned to the House of Commons. It was agreed to recommended an immediate payment of £350 towards Sykes's total debts of £778-10s-3d, with the balance to be paid later. It also asked the Committee for the Advance of Money to secure his release from prison. On 2 August the Lords and Commons assembled in Parliament agreed the payment of £350 and endorsed the request to the Committee to help Sykes in his captivity.

We do not know if Sykes received his money or when he was released from prison. However, the story did not have a happy ending.

In 1652 William Sykes was the parish constable of Knottingley near Leeds. He had formed links with the Quaker movement and had also opposed the collection of tithes, which he believed was contrary to the teachings of the gospel. He also urged others in the parish not to pay.

The local clergy was far from happy with this act of defiance and in August 1652 he was prosecuted and fined a total of £266-13s-4d. Unable to pay, Sykes was incarcerated in York Castle, where he died on 20 October.

EXTRACTS FROM THE GAINSBOROUGH PARISH BURIAL RECORDS FOR 1643

1643	Juley 18	3 Captains with 3 more shouldgers that was slane
1643	Juley 21	3 Souldgers
1643	Juley 22	3 Souldgers
1643	Juley 25	2 Souldgers
1643	Juley 28	3 Souldgers Slaine
1643	Juley 28	Thomas Atkinson slain a Souldier born at Rippon
1643	Juley 30	Coronall Candey (Colonel Cavendish) slane heare and Buried at Newarke
1643	Juley 30	4 Souldgers
1643	Auguste 1	6 Souldgers
1643	Auguste 2	4 Souldgers

RECOMMENDED READING

A Book of Gainsborough by Ian Beckwith. Barracuda Books. 1988.
An excellent history of the town from earliest times.

Gainsborough During the Great Civil War by Ian Beckwith. 1969.
A short history of the Civil War and its effects on the town.

Gainsborough Through Time by Sally Outram. Amberley Publishing.
2012.
A photographic history of the town's buildings and landmarks.

All Saints, Gainsborough by Jane Veale. MK Digital Print, Gainsborough.
2012 edition.
A history and guide devoted to Gainsborough's parish church.

Oliver Cromwell and the Battle of Gainsborough by John West. Richard
Kay. 1992.
A look into the battle and the career of Oliver Cromwell.

Other titles of interest.

Oliver Cromwell by Martyn Bennett. Routledge Historical Biographies.
2006.
There are many biographies of Cromwell but this is one of the best.

Cromwell at War: The Lord General and his Military Revolution by Martyn Bennett. I.B. Tauris. 2017.
The definitive study of Cromwell's military career.

The A to Z of the British and Irish Civil Wars 1637-1660 by Martyn Bennett. Scarecrow Press. 2010.
An essential reference work for all those interested in the period.

Travellers' Guide to the Battlefields of the English Civil War by Martyn Bennett. Michael Joseph. 1990.
An excellent guide to the battles of the English Civil War.

Our Chief of Men by Lady Antonia Fraser. W&N. 2008 edition.
First published in the 1970s but still the definitive biography of Oliver Cromwell.

The English Civil War – A Military History by Dr Peter Gaunt. I.B. Tauris. 2017.
A comprehensive study of the war.

Seventeenth-Century Lincolnshire by Clive Holmes. History of Lincolnshire Committee. 1980.
A history of the county in the seventeenth century. Includes chapters on the English Civil War and Protectorate.

ABOUT THE AUTHOR

JOHN WEST was born in Edmonton, North London. He now lives in Suffolk. He is a film producer, actor, award-winning DJ and TV presenter and is the author of books and articles on history, crime, ghosts and folklore. One of his guides, *Roman Lincoln*, was turned into a *BBC Radio Lincolnshire* documentary. Other books include studies of Roman York, Oliver Cromwell and Victorian murders. His first book on British ghosts **Britain's Haunted Heritag**e – was published by JMD Media in November 2019.

As a journalist, John has written for magazines including *Psychic News* and *Suffolk and Norfolk Life*. His features have ranged from celebrity interviews to investigations of famous hauntings from the UK and beyond. He has worked as a presenter at six radio stations, including *BBC Radio Suffolk*, and has several hundred shows to his credit.

John was *Mustard TV's* regular studio historian for over three years and appeared on the Norfolk station to talk about subjects ranging from the Romans to The Beatles. He was also a guest on London Live TV where he discussed the photographer and author Simon Marsden and Jason Figgis's film about his life and work.

John was a supporting artist on BBC's *Detectorists,* Netflix's *The Crown,* and feature films, *The Personal History of David Copperfield, Grandest Wedding of Royals* and Danny Boyle's *Yesterday.*

He has been interviewed on *BBC Cornwall, BBC Essex, BBC Norfolk, BBC Suffolk, BBC Lincolnshire, KCOR Radio, RWSfm, Felixstowe Radio, Felixstowe TV, Blythe Radio, Siren Radio, ICR, Deben Radio, Blog Talk Radio, IO Radio* and *Minster FM* about his books and his interest in history, film and folklore. He has been the subject of articles in several newspapers and magazines concerning his books and interest in ghosts and history.

In 2018 John teamed up with film and TV writer/director Jason Figgis. He became a producer/publicist on the film, *Simon Marsden: A Life in Pictures,* going on to produce and act in Figgis' M.R. James inspired chiller *Winifred Meeks.* Other productions from the team include *The Grey Man, Clare Island, The Wedding Ring, In Our Day, Mythmaker: George A. Romero, The Black Widow* and *Dunkirk 80.* Several other film and documentary projects with Figgis are now in pre-production.

John is also a photographer with work featured in newspapers and magazines across the UK. His first photographic exhibition was held in Suffolk in 2017.

ND - #0330 - 270225 - C0 - 234/156/7 - PB - 9781780916187 - Gloss Lamination